NASHO DAZE

THE LIGHTER SIDE OF NATIONAL SERVICE

First published 2011

ISBN: 9781921555978

Cover design by Watson Ferguson & Company.

Published by Boolarong Press, Salisbury, Brisbane, Australia.

Printed and bound by Watson Ferguson & Company, Salisbury, Brisbane, Australia.

Dedicated to the 287,000 young men called up for National Service in the Navy, Army and Air Force between 1951 and 1972.

60th Anniversary of National Service 2011

4

7

8

9

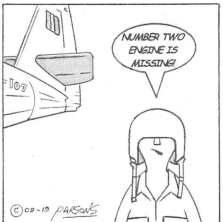

HOME SWEET HOME

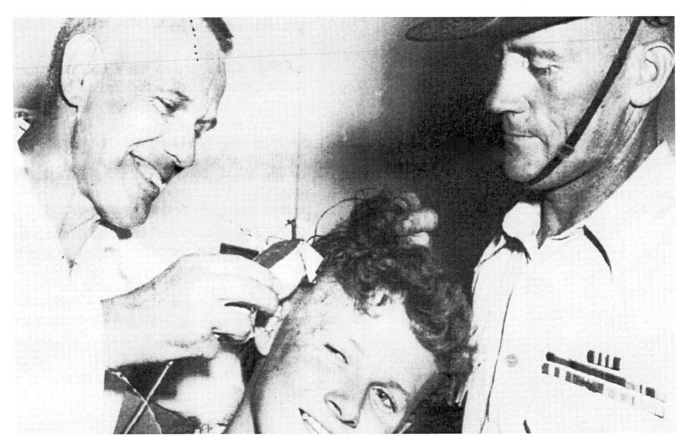

VE HAVE VAYS TO MAKE YOU TALK

DONT EVEN THINK ABOUT IT

WILL THAT BE CASH OR CREDIT, SIR?

JUDSON PHOTO

WOT, NO BAR?

WINTER WOOLLIES

JOLLY JACK TARS

CRUISE THE PACIFIC ABOARD
RAN LINE'S LUXURIOUS HMAS MELBOURNE
AUST. WAR MEMORIAL PHOTO

21

SAY "CHEESE"

NASHO PHOTO

I CAN'T HEAR YOU WITH ALL THAT NOISE

CLEAN UP DAY

QUICK, WHERE'S THE PORTALOO MATE?

F. PETERSON PHOTO

27

29

Australia had made training in the Citizens Military Force compulsory at various times between 1910 and 1945 and the 1951 National Service Act revived this with army national servicemen completing their obligation in the CMF.

In the 1970s the CMF was reorganised as the Ready Reserve and then the Army Reserve. The Citizens Air Force became the Air Force Reserve. The Naval Reserve remained virtually unchanged. In 2001 the Defence Act was amended so that Reservists could be called up for overseas service.

Despite the compulsion, national servicemen of both schemes did their training, active and reserve duties well and honourably and most regarded it as a rewarding part of their lives. They served overseas with distinction in Vietnam, Malaysia, Borneo and Papua-New Guinea.

These were the principal reasons why the Australian Government recognised the contribution of national servicemen to Australia's defence preparedness with the award in 2001 of the Anniversary of National Service 1951-1972 Medal. The bronze medal is unusual in modern awards with a double-sided design and the recipient's service number and name engraved on the rim.

The front depicts the tri-service badge surmounted by the Federation star and the words "Anniversary of National Service 1951-1972" and the other side the Southern Cross on a field of radiating lines inside a cog wheel representing the integral role of the armed services in the Australian community. Both sides are surmounted by the Crown. The distinctive ribbon uses the colours of the three services during the National Service era – navy white, army jungle green and air force light blue – and Australia's then national colours of blue and gold. The ochre strip represents the land.

Because National Service was drawn from the entire community, many national servicemen from both schemes later rose to high positions in politics, business, the professions and the community.

All national servicemen are ex-servicemen. Those who served overseas are returned servicemen. They march on ANZAC Day, Remembrance Day, National Service Day, Vietnam Veterans and Long Tan Days and Reserve Forces Day in their own right. No women were called up for National Service.

National servicemen marched as a contingent in the army's Centenary Parade in Canberra in 2001. They wear a wide variety of service and corps badges on their hats, caps and berets and many are members of unit associations in all three services.

The National Servicemen's Association of Australia was founded in Toowoomba, Queensland, in 1987 by the late Barry Vicary, a 1960s national serviceman, to seek a better deal for Vietnam-era national servicemen who had served in support units in Australia and Malaysia. When he learnt of the earlier and larger National Service scheme he immediately widened the organisation to include them. The Association now has branches Australia-wide and is the second-largest ex-service organization after the RSL.

National servicemen added a new word to the Australian language – Nasho. National Service Day, 14 February, marks the day the last Nasho marched out of camp.

NATIONAL SERVICEMEN'S ASSOCIATION OF AUSTRALIA STATE HEADQUARTERS

National Servicemen's Assoc'n of Aust. (NSW Branch) Inc.

P.O. Box 126 BELFIELD, NSW 2191

Ph (02) 9759 3629

Email webmaster@nasho.asn.au

www.nasho.asn.au

National Servicemen's Assoc'n of Aust. (Victorian Branch) Inc.

P.O. Box 44 PORTLAND, Vic 3305

Ph (03) 5523 3329

Email valmaym1@ozemail.com.au

http://nashos.org.au/~vic

National Servicemen's Assoc'n of Aust. (Qld) Inc.

P.O. Box 7014 HOLLAND PARK EAST, Qld 4121

Ph (07) 3324 1277

Email nashosqld@gmail.com

www.nashoqld.org.au

National Servicemen's Assoc'n of Aust. South Australian Branch

G.P.O. Box 388 ADELAIDE, SA 5001

Ph (08) 8293 6344

Email nsaasa@adam.com.au

www.nashossa.org.au

National Servicemen's Assoc'n of Aust. W.A. Branch

19 Brailsford Way BUTLER, W.A. 6036

Ph (08) 9562 1502

Email brianandbarb@westnet.com.au

http://nashos.org.au/~wa

National Servicemen's Assoc'n of Aust. (Tasmania) Inc.

Ph Roy Payne (03) 6423 4033

http://nashos.org.au/~tas

National Servicemen's Assoc'n of Aust. A.C.T. Branch

P.O. Box 7211 DUFFY, ACT 2611

Ph (02) 6288 8993

Email nashos@incanberra.com.au

www.nationalservicecanberra.com

National Servicemen's Assoc'n of Aust. Northern Territory (Inc)

P.O. Box 904 NIGHTCLIFF, NT 0814

Ph (08) 8948 5556

Email icdawalsh@bigpond.com

http://nashos.org.au/~qld/darwin.htm